DES PLAINES
RIVER
ANTHOLOGY

THE HISTORICAL SOCIETY OF FOREST PARK

The Historical Society of Forest Park
Forest Park, IL
forestparkhistory.org

in association with
Allium Press of Chicago
Forest Park, IL
alliumpress.com

Project Team:

August Aleksy
Amy Binns-Calvey
Diane Grah
Jean Lotus
Emily Clark Victorson

Book and cover design by E. C. Victorson
Title page original artwork by John Lotus

Trade Paperback ISBN: 978-0-9890535-1-8

TABLE OF CONTENTS

INTRODUCTION

There were two sources of inspiration for this work. Naturally, there was my high school reading of Edgar Lee Masters's *Spoon River Anthology* and its annual performance by teachers and professors at the college I attended. The other source was the Village of Forest Park centennial celebration held in 2007. As I helped at the Historical Society's table, on the fields of Altenheim, I had an enlightening experience, learning about the multitude of cemeteries that are contained within the borders of our town. Citizens of the community bragged to me about the many famous, infamous, and "ordinary" victims who are laid to eternal rest in these burial grounds. The two pieces came together in my mind and I considered that it would be a great wedding of literature and history, if done in the proper fashion.

In my experience as a bookseller I've met many excellent authors who've written about these individuals within their books. I thought, *Why not ask them to each write a short, first-person soliloquy about that character, in a style comparable to that of Edgar Lee Masters?*

I was a little nervous, but enthusiastic, and, it seems, the authors sensed that. 99% of those I approached agreed to participate on a pro bono basis, in support of the Historical Society. They shared in my vision of this as a literary work and wrote some of the best pieces of prose, in this style, that I have read. Some became so caught up in the project that they wrote multiple pieces.

I am not a writer or grammarian by trade, so I solicited the wholehearted support of two local people—one, our newspaper editor and, the other, the publisher of a local literary press. There were no prima donnas among the contributors—they were all gracious participants in the editorial process.

Along with my dream for this printed opus, I thought, *Wouldn't it be great to also transform it into a dramatic performance, as my teachers did at college?* As I shared this idea with one of my customers, he mentioned that his wife was professionally involved in the local theater scene. After some gentle persuasion, she volunteered her services, along with those of the fellow performers she "strong-armed" to participate.

Now this book is in your hands for enjoyment, education, and enlightenment. Isn't it amazing that a literary endeavor like this—about mortals—could help immortalize them?

Thank you to all the contributors, and to you, for supporting the Historical Society of Forest Park.

August Aleksy
President
The Historical Society of Forest Park

Resting Along the River

Emily Victorson

Where are Clarence, Belle, Mike, Justin and Mary,
The physician, the temptress, the celebrity, the young lovers?
All, all are sleeping by the river.

One took his own life,
One took many lives with her.
One was lost in the sky,
Two were lost in the icy depths.
All, all are sleeping, sleeping, sleeping by the river.

Where are Caroline and Grace, Albert and Lucy,
The Kettlestrings, the Potawatomi,
The frustrated, the determined, the pioneers, the pushed aside?
All, all are sleeping by the river.

Two sang in their dreams,
Two dreamt of a better world,
Two settled here before there was a town,
And then there were those,
Who were here before the rest.
All, all are sleeping, sleeping, sleeping by the river.

Where are Abraham, Eddie, Billy, Maria, and Philander,
The Bible saver, the jazz man, the evangelist,
The gypsy, the chronicler?
All, all are sleeping by the river.

One fought for the Union,
One went to Spain to fight for independence,
One thumped a mitt and then a Bible,
One succumbed to the flu,
One peddled, then snapped.
All, all are sleeping, sleeping, sleeping by the river.

Where are Adolph, Emma, Clara and Bill,
The sausage maker, the Earth mother,
The feisty lady, the Union man?
All, all are sleeping by the river.

One ground up his wife,
One fought for her beliefs,
One attained fame for a phrase,
One is only half here.
All, all are sleeping, sleeping, sleeping by the river.

Where are the druids, the circus folk, the Haymarket martyrs,
The fraternal, the entertainers, the agitators?
All, all are sleeping by the river.

One group is buried in circles,
One rests beneath monumental elephants,
One is the final destination of May's pilgrims.
All, all are sleeping, sleeping, sleeping by the river.

James Justin & Mary Manthey
Jay Bonansinga

We don't have much time.
They don't dole out these moments lightly.
Once in a generation, I reckon, it comes like a whisper.
Like a single heartbeat on the wind.
As the sun melts over the babbling Des Plaines.
And the breeze rattles the wrought iron gates,
And the tops of the twisted, twined trees that line the cemetery.
We get to stand in the fading light of a spring day.
We get to breathe the clover-perfumed air.
And tell our story.

Oh…forgive me.
Allow me to introduce the lovely lass at my side.
This is Mary Manthey.
Still as comely and handsome as the day she turned twenty-two.
In her ivory taffeta dress and her crinoline bonnet,
She's a pretty one…ain't she?

That's how it works, you see.
Death takes you in a blink.
But you stay who you are for about a thousand eternities.
I should warn you, though…
Mary here's a shy one.
It is her custom to allow me to do the speaking…
So I reckon I will.

Ah...almost forgot.

Name's James Justin. Call me Jim.

Still twenty years old to this day.

Line worker by trade.

Last employed by Western Electric, Hawthorne Works,

Cicero, Illinois.

Shoulders are still broad from the work I suppose.

Hands still a tad scabrous and calloused,

From handling Bakelite housings,

For that new-fangled gizmo

Came to be known as the telephone.

Guess I should get to the point.

Mary here always says I need to come to the point quicker.

People got things to do, places to be.

We was engaged to be married when it happened.

Ain't that right, Mary?

As I said, she's a meek one,

Don't talk too much.

I knew she was the one for me, though.

The instant she came in the lunchroom,

Back around ought-twelve.

Our eyes met.

And...I saw them sweet cornflower baby blues...

And...and my heart it...

I can't think about that now.

Got something to tell.

Thing is, it happened in a blink.

The bad thing.

We was all set to ride the big boat called the *Eastland.*

Had our picnic basket up there on the promenade with us.

Sweet tea and biscuits in there, I think it was...

Wasn't it, Mary?

All dressed up to the nines we was.

Up on the top deck in the wind.
Waving to people.
Ain't got around to getting our wedding rings yet,
But we was proud...I'll tell you that...
And we was in love,
And looking forward to a day across the Lake,
A parade over there by Michigan City.

When all of a sudden,
Without one whit of a warning,
There was a shrieking noise,
Wood and metal wrenching,
And the big boat took a lurch and tipped over,
And tossed us all in the dirty drink.
Darkness and cold and the stink of the greasy water
Took our lives.
And Mary and me died like the day we fell in love,
Hand-in-hand, together, as one,
In the freezing blackness of oblivion.

Calm down, Mary-Girl.
The telling's almost over...it's alright.
She's caught a bit a chill, you see.
Let me put my coat over her for a second. There.
I don't think I want to talk about this no more.

That's how it works.
You see...death takes you in a blink.
But I ain't going to think about that right now.
I'm going to think about another blink of an eye,
That changes everything...
That lasts for a lifetime of eternities...
That cannot be erased.

I'm gonna think about that day back in 1912,
In the lunchroom at Hawthorne,
Standing over by the water tank,
When I saw her come through that door,
When my heart swelled and my mouth went dry,
And I fell like a ton of bricks for my sweet Mary.

It happens in the blink of an eye.
Love...
And eternal sleep, side by side,
With my gal, my bride-to-be, my everything,
My dear lovely Mary Manthey.

Song of the Potawatomi

Kathryn Atwood and Donald Perrot

We are the counselors, the keepers of fire,
Who live in a land that is good.
We fish in the river, we plant in the ground,
And we hunt for our food in the woods.
We travel away to the land by the lake—
Eshkago, the place of the swamp.
We meet the white man,
Who is there with his goods,
And we trade with him what he wants.

Our daughters we marry to Kchemok, our friend.
But soon other white men come near,
And tell us we cannot continue in peace,
With the white men who live at the fort.

These words found a place in the heart and the mind,
Of some of our own young braves.
Fear was grown thick at Fort Dearborn,
And plans were made to leave.

Promise was made of food, drink, and guns,
All that the fort could supply,
If we would just help the frightened whites leave,
Led safely by our side.

But the promise was broken, an ambush was laid.
We killed and we rescued, we kidnapped the whites—
The whites who were ever our friend.
Kchemok, who is always our friend.

White settlers came in, they were stealing the homes,
From the Sauk, Fox, and Winnebago,
Who were told that they'd promised their land to the whites,
A very long time ago.

Black Hawk, our brother, was right to return,
To the land that was truly his home,
And he asked us to help him to fight the white man.
Shabbonah, our leader, said no.

We would never raise up the tomahawk high,
Against Kchemok, the white man, our friend,
And some of us helped him defeat Black Hawk's cause,
And his war came to a sad end.

Then Kchemok took our own land away,
And exchanged it for money and drink.
He gave our sons whiskey, put quills in their hands,
And told them that they had to leave.

Our sons could not leave, without saying goodbye.
They must honor our Mother, this land.
They asked the Great Spirits to bless all who leave,
And to watch over we who remain.

They grieved much to leave our bones buried here,
And these are the words that they cried:
"Great Spirits, protect us! Great land, don't forget us!
Precious bones, we will meet you again!"

The road they must travel is bitter and cold.
They must dress so that they will have strength,
To find their new homes at the end of the road,
The land Kchemok said they could have.

The sky will be their home until then,
As they travel this unknown path,
Away from the land that we once called our home.
That we shared with Kchemok our friend.
The white man who once was our friend,
The white man who once was our friend.

Joseph and Betty Kettlestrings
D. M. Pirrone

Joseph

I came from Yorkshire in 1831.
England's washed up, I said. America beckoned—
So Betty and I, my lovely bride, we came.
To the brawling, bustling cities of this new place:
Baltimore, Cincinnati.
Noisy, crowded cities, teeming with chances.
For work, for money; to strive, to build.
For a carpenter with a wife and young ones to feed.
And then Chicago, "where the streets are gold!"
Or so they said. And so we went,
We four and one coming, across the wilderness.
Like Joseph of old and his wife, also with child,
Pilgrims in a rattletrap horse-drawn wagon.
And there on the horizon, by the river,
On the bank of the Des Plaines, where now we slumber,
Oak trees! Tall and straight, seen for miles,
Sentinels of higher ground. Of civilization.
I bought land cheap, sold it for far better.
The wild gave way to houses, schools, and churches.
We became the Kettlestrings, founders of a town.
A town, where once was nothing
But wilderness and pluck and stubborn hope.

♦

Betty

Swamp land, that's all there was, swamp and mud.
Mosquitoes, Indian country, and bad roads.
Civilization is where people are.
Or where they might come, given reason.
Where they did come, off the stagecoach and the trains.
To the Oak Ridge Hotel at Kettlestrings Grove.
A little house Joseph built, with boards that warped
And let in the winter's chill.
Did the cold damp take our little Ellen
Out there on the Illinois prairie? I never knew.
Hard work brought us healing of a sort.
Cooking, cleaning, raising more children.
I birthed eleven all in all;
But only five outlived me.
That August in Chicago, scarlet fever,
Anne, Mary, Thomas, all three gone.
Our family headstone stands, but it's in me;
Their names engraved forever in my heart.

Caroline Hancock Hall

Carol Hauswald

I told you, daughter,
"Tend to your practicing.
There is no use any woman
Getting into the kitchen if she can help it."

But you married Clarence anyway.
Turning your back on singing contralto,
At the Metropolitan Opera.

Ah, that night, that glorious night,
You sang at Madison Square Garden.
Had a contract all but signed.
Remember the song we wrote together,
"God laid me aside to rest me"?

I rest now in my restless state,
Daughter of an English sea captain.
"But the night seemed rather long.
So I grieved and I wept for the morning.
Confusing the right and the wrong."

What went wrong, child?
It was my sickness wasn't it?
The boy in the clapboard house,
Tended to me,
When I was dying.

And you both talked,
And talked into the night.
He fell in love with your voice.
My voice,
My dream.

Clarence, the doctor,
A man of science,
Keeper of strange, wet things,
In jars on shelves.
What did you love about that boy?

No matter now,
I sang soprano and painted landscapes,
And the glorious admirers came in waves,
Overflowing the Oak Park pond
With applause.

Grace Hall Hemingway
Carol Hauswald

I did practice, Mama. I did.
Madam Louisa Cappiani prepared me well for that night.
The night I sang contralto at Madison Square Garden,
And was offered a contract to join the Met.

But the lights, the footlights were so bright!
They blinded me, Mama,
Just like the scarlet fever,
That left me blind for a while.
And then the migraines started.
I could not sign the contract,
The lights were so bright!

But I remember the sweet song we wrote,
"But when at morn he woke me,
As a loving father would,
I repented my rebellion,
And only saw the good."
I repented, Mama.

I married Clarence,
But sang and painted,
And taught others to sing.
I even designed the house,
A scaled-down Metropolitan Opera.
With a grand piano and recital space,
And even a separate entrance,
Separate from Clarence's patients and Indian artifacts.

Dr. Clarence Hemingway
Kenneth J. Knack

Dr. Clarence Hemingway was my name.
As a physician,
I vowed to preserve life,
Yet took my own.
The instrument...my father's Civil War pistol.

Although Oak Park was my home,
My office was once housed,
In the Forest Park State Bank building,
The building standing there today.

Along the banks of the Des Plaines River,
My son Ernest used to hunt and play.
Not far from where I now reside,
Alongside my wife Grace,
In my forest home.

Ernest became an author,
A talent unto itself.
His mother, the accomplished singer,
Dabbled in oil painting from time to time.
Ernest got his creativity from her...
But his love for hunting, and the outdoors, from me.

I wish Ernest had chosen
A different epilogue to his life story,
Than that of his sister Ursula, brother Leicester, and I.
There is suspicion that hemochromatosis is to blame.

The disease causes toxic levels of iron,
To accumulate in the joints and organs,
Bringing pain, diabetes, cirrhosis of the liver,
Heart disease and depression.

I myself suffered from diabetes and heart disease,
So, at fifty-seven,
I decided to end my suffering.
I often wonder
Why Grace had the Bible passage, John 15:13,
Inscribed upon my stone.
"Greater love has no one than this,
That he lay down his life for his friends."
For I laid down my life for myself.

Abraham Van Schoick
John Rice

See this Bible?
I carried it in my front pocket,
All through the Civil War.
No holes in it,
But I believe it still protected me.
It couldn't save my father,
Or other fellows in the unit.

Dr. William Van Schoick was my father.
A wealthy man, he was German,
But loved his new country.
He gave the government $10,000 in gold pieces,
To buy shoes for the Union boys.
He later gave much more.

I was born on Groundhog Day, 1836,
In Narrowsburg, New York.
I had a brother, Benjamin.
Before the war, we worked in the construction business.
We were mustered into the 15th New York at Port Jervis.

My father joined our unit
As a physician and surgeon.
He set up his headquarters, in Marshville, Tennessee,
To treat the wounded.
He caught the undulant fever and died.
They shipped his body back to the family cemetery.

Many of our boys died from fever.
Our regiment lost one hundred twenty-nine during the war,
One hundred fifteen to disease.
I stayed healthy, though,
And they put me in charge of a construction crew,
To rebuild the bridges the Confederates burned down.

Our regiment was attached to the Army of the Potomac.
We went ahead of the troops to rebuild the bridges.
We started in 1861, constructing spans,
Across the Chickahominy in Maryland.

We were involved in every major battle:
Fredericksburg, Chancellorsville and Gettysburg.
We built the siege works
Used against Petersburg and Richmond.
We kept at it until Appomattox.

I was mustered out on July 2, 1865,
And headed west.
I married Jennie,
And we had Mae, Dora, Henry, William, and Sam.
I drove a streetcar.
I was a card-carrying member of Local 308,
The Amalgamated Association of Street and Electric Railways.
I was retired when we moved to Forest Park.
It was 1908 and we lived at 635 Beloit.

What a garden I had!
People came from miles to see it.
I was still tending it at ninety-two,
Never sick a day of my life.
But I started feeling poorly on December 21, 1928.
Five days later I was dead.
Left behind Jennie, my grown-up kids,
And this Bible.

My granddaughter, Zita,
Held onto my Bible for seventy-five years.
When she became the first treasurer
Of the Forest Park Historical Society
She donated it to the collection.
Inside the cover, it says I carried it through the war.
A bullet never found it.

Philander Walker Barclay
Sheila Reynolds Trainor

I'm Philander Barclay,
And let's get to the name first thing,
So that we can move on.
Yes, it meant the same thing then as it does now.
No, I never did meet another person—ever,
With my name.
What were my parents thinking? you may ask.
I have no idea,
As it was not a topic for discussion.

But it's not as if they were highfalutin people—
My father ran a drug store on Marion Street.
Maybe they wanted to sound a bit grander than they were,
So they slapped me with a fancy,
But sturdy-sounding, name.
All I know is that I was always "Philander" in the house,
No nicknames allowed.

I will tell you that I fell in love with Oak Park and River Forest,
Almost from the day my family moved here in 1890,
When I was twelve years old.
I've heard that some people thought it was sleepy around here,
But it was much more exciting than my birthplace,
Anna, Illinois.
What's that? You say you never heard of it?
I rest my case.
Of course, everything's relative, as they say.

Photographs have interested me
For as far back as I can remember.
The idea of capturing, freezing, a moment in time
Fascinates me.
I started collecting other peoples' pictures first.
Sometimes I'd find them,
While I was riding my bike around town,
Posted on store bulletin boards and such.
What I really wanted was my own camera.
That had to wait, however, as I was kept busy,
Working at my ma and pa's drugstore,
The very distinguished sounding "Sign of the Golden Lion."

A bigger draw than the pharmaceuticals,
Was the fact that the establishment,
Held the license for one of the first telephones in Oak Park.
My parents, James and Mary, took messages,
And I would bike around town to deliver them.
There's some people say I'd read those messages on the way,
Just to keep up on village news.
Maybe I did, maybe I didn't.

Thing is, I loved my village
And did like to know what was going on.
But, the truth is, I never really developed the knack,
For getting close to people.
So any gossip was safe with me.
With money from working at my dad's store,
Finally, I got my first camera.
Nothing fancy, a black Kodak box.
But it served its purpose very well.

I fancied myself a photo historian
Of my little piece of the world.
Someday it would all be changed,
And I figured people would be glad to have my pictures,

To remember how it was.
So I'd pedal all around,
Taking pictures of whatever struck my fancy:
Buildings, lots of those, railroads, houses,
And sometimes even people.

I must say that the fellow residents of my two little towns,
Seemed to enjoy them.
Eventually, I moved around the corner from the drugstore,
And started my own business, repairing bikes.
It was a pleasant enough occupation,
But the role of historic preservationist,
Through photography, that was my passion.

Sadly, so was my need for drugs
Like morphine and sleeping powders (both legal then).
I started using innocently in my youth,
But that habit gradually grew into the scourge of addiction.
I died too soon, at the age of sixty-two.
Memories of my free-roaming days,
Riding through my lovely villages,
Snapping pictures for posterity,
Would sometimes rise up through my clouded consciousness,
Visions at once both pleasing and torturous.
I could no longer live the life required of one tethered to,
And completely overcome by, the drug demons.
I made my way into Chicago one day,
(I was much too fond of my hometowns to end things here),
Found a hotel, and there finally found peace.

Despite my final despair, I felt good about one thing:
By the time of my death,
I had accumulated about one thousand images of our villages.
And I hear that they're being preserved for the future—
My life's work hasn't been forgotten.
In fact, my photos are still on view at the Historical Society.

It's nice to know that villagers can always be reminded
That at the turn of the nineteenth century,
Much of the place was still rural,
So rural that there were cows grazing in front yards!

Oh, sorry, wait…if I might add one more thing.
While I was never really a "joiner,"
I did help organize a group of "old timers,"
Who would sit around and share tales at the Harness Shop.
Oral history is priceless, too, to my mind.
We called it "The Borrowed Time Club."
(Nothing grim about that.)
Only men over seventy could join.

I hear tell that the club still exists today,
Though the name's been changed.
I do hope they've loosened the age and gender limits by now…
I can only imagine the wider range of stories with women,
And a variety of adult ages included.
No one person could ramble on too long and, who knows,
Perhaps an occasional photo might even show up,
To be added to my collection.
A man can dream, can't he?

Belle Gunness
Richard Lindberg

I was born in 1859,
On a farm in Selbu,
Near the fjords of northern Norway.
My real name is Brynhilde Poulsdatter Storseth,
But that doesn't matter now.
History remembers me as Belle Gunness.
You better remember that too,
Because I am well known in these parts,
And what I did to a collection of gullible men,
Are among the most violent acts,
You can conjure up in your nightmares…
If you dare.
A hint: I gutted them like an animal!

I was the daughter of a peasant farmer and stone mason.
Times were hard.
There was no money,
And I was but a mere girl,
Working as a dairy maid and cattle girl—
Someone who led the livestock to the pastures to feed.
It was dirty, nasty work,
And the young people called me
"Snurk-vist-pala," meaning "little twigs."
They were cruel, they were mean, and I hated them.

When I was seventeen
I was assaulted by a man
And put in the family way.
The rogue!

He did not abide me,
And left me to suffer scandal and humiliation.
An unmarried girl of seventeen,
With child in those days!
Imagine it!

At a country dance one night,
I met a wealthy young man.
I thought he liked me.
But, like most men, he wanted something—
More of me than I would give.
When I resisted, he hit me.
He kicked me in the abdomen.
I was severely hurt and I lost the baby.

I was determined to leave this place,
Of misery and wretchedness.
I saved my money and, in 1881,
Moved to the Logan Square neighborhood of Chicago,
To live with my sister Nellie.
I found peace there…for a time.
I married Mads Sorensen,
A department store watchman, in 1884,
And we lived as man and wife.
We bought a grocery store on the West Side.
I served the children candy.
Oh, how I loved children,
Although I could not have any of my own.
I took in the young ones,
And cared for them,
And loved them and fed them.

Sometimes I brought in a baby no-one wanted,
And told the prying neighbors of Austin,
That the child was my own.
There were four of them.

The fools believed it.
Well, some of them did, at any rate.
The rest, well, they wondered
Why a woman of middle age,
Who was childless for eleven years of married life,
Would suddenly deliver four in three years.
They accused me of running a baby farm,
And called me a woman of low character.
But I don't care about the nosey neighbors.

The little ones died,
And so did my poor besotted husband.
Stomach troubles, it was.
I was tired of him,
And the insurance money I collected,
Got me away from the snoopy neighbors in Austin.
Oh, it was so easy to get away with it!
A little arsenic here and little arsenic there—
I stirred it into my home cooking that Mads loved so well,
And the coppers were never the wiser.
What possible reason
Would compel a kindly middle-aged woman
To murder a husband of fourteen years?
Hmmmm??

With my money I bought a farm,
Outside La Porte, Indiana.
I married Peter Gunness,
A widower, who was a lodger
Living under our roof in Austin.
I think Mads would have approved of our nuptials!
Such a nice man!
But tragedy seemed to follow me everywhere!
My Goodness!

In 1902, poor Peter was sitting at my kitchen table
And an anvil fell on his head from an overhead shelf!
How could that have happened?
I will confess to you now for the first time…
That it wasn't really on the shelf after all,
But in my firm grasp.
If I got away with murder once,
Why not twice,
Why not forty times?

New to this game,
But wise to the vanities of desperate, lonely men—
Looking for a nice lady, good home cooking,
And a wonderful home life—
I placed notices in the Scandinavian newspapers.
The lonely hearts game they called it,
And one by one,
From all over the Midwest,
They came to meet me,
To romance me, and to sample
My old-fashioned country steak, sweet cakes, and coffee.
Once I had their money deposited in my bank
The arsenic and the plant poisons did the rest.
Oh, how I remember the anguish on their faces!
Men! They had it coming!

In the basement I cut them up.
I knew the butcher's trade
And I took a blade to them.
The body parts were much enjoyed
By the swine on my pig farm.
The men were mostly lonely bachelors without family.
In those days,
If a man in those circumstances went missing,
No-one much cared.

So it went on for eight years, until 1908,
When I done away with Andrew Helgelein,
Gave him an appropriate burial,
And counted my money.
That is until his brother, Asle,
Announced his intention to come to La Porte,
To inquire after his missing brother.
The fool did not believe me
When I told him that Andrew and me did not get along
And that he had gone off to the West,
To seek his fortune.

What was I to do?
I made a hasty decision.
I burned my house down,
Killed the two children
And a woman I hired from Chicago to work as my cook.
I cut off her head
And left the remains where they were—
In the basement.
I fled Indiana,
And the infamy I left behind,
Confused and baffled the police,
As I knew it would.
Who was this headless victim?
Me, Belle Gunness, or a body double?
To this day, they do not know,
Even with their fancy modern forensics and gee-gaws!
So where am I?

Adolph Louis Luetgert

Robert Loerzel

As long as I live,
I will be pointed out as the sausage-maker who killed his wife,
Even if she should come to the jail
And take me out this afternoon.
This is one of the hardest things to bear.
Yes, that's him—that's the one,
That's Adolph Louis Luetgert.

I was born in Germany.
I lived like any other boy.
I came to this country when I was twenty-four years of age,
Ignorant of the ways of the world.
I was lured from my peaceful German village,
By the stories I heard,
About this "land of the free and home of the brave."

I came to Chicago, where I knew not a soul.
I had three cents.
I worked early and late.
I saved my money.
I started in the sausage business in a very modest way,
But I devoted all of my time and energies to it.

I succeeded in devising special processes.
I could manufacture sausages in summer as well as in winter,
Something that no one else in the world could do.
This gave me prestige and brought me wealth.

It was said that I was proud, haughty, and arrogant.
All because I did not associate much with my neighbors.
But the truth is,
I was too hard at work to bother with such diversions.

My wife, Louisa, and I lived happily together.
Until recently, when I had financial trouble.
She was mad at me for losing my money.
She thought I was going to lose the business.
She was afraid people would laugh at us.
I told her, "Let them laugh."
She said, "I won't stay in Chicago,
And have people pointing fingers at me."
She said she was going away.

The last time I saw Louisa was the night of May 1, 1897,
In our house on Diversey.
She was sitting in the kitchen.
She was reading a newspaper,
Under the gaslight near the stove.
And then I went over to the factory.
I spent the night making some soap in the basement.
The next morning, Louisa was gone.

I don't know where she is.
As soon as she arrives,
All of these charges against me will be cleared up.
The police say I murdered her.
They found a few pieces of bone inside my sausage factory.
They say I dissolved her body in a vat.
It's all nonsense.
They locked me up in Cook County Jail,
Separating me from our two young boys.

The newspapers of Chicago have been notoriously unfair.
If I was pale,
They said it was a sign of guilt.
If I retained my usual complexion,
They said I was brazen.
If I smiled,
They said I was hysterical.
If I seemed despondent,
They said I was breaking down.

They have published pictures of my eyes,
My nose, my ears, my mouth,
My teeth and my hair.
All so horribly distorted.
Those who do not know me,
Must have suspected that I was a monster.
Everything that a man says or does,
When he is charged with crime,
Is said to be an evidence of guilt.
Some of the papers said I was indifferent
When the bones were brought into the courtroom.
They commented on the way I examined the bones,
And smelled them.

But I knew they weren't the bones of my wife.
I knew the police were manufacturing evidence against me.
I knew those bones were hog and sheep bones.
Why shouldn't I examine them with indifference,
And with considerable amusement?
Ever since I was arrested,
I have gone to bed at night and slept,
As quietly, peacefully, and innocently as a child.
Why should I worry?
I've done nothing that I'm ashamed of.

But after two trials, a jury found me guilty.
Sentenced me to life in prison.
I say to you:
I am as innocent of this crime as you are!
If the men on that jury believed I am guilty,
They should have hanged me.
When they gave me neither death nor liberty,
They proved they were cowards.
I laughed at the verdict.
It was foolishness.

As to my poor wife,
God only knows where she is.
I am afraid she is wandering about,
In a distracted condition,
In utter ignorance of the fact that
Her disappearance has caused me to lose everything.
I trust that a just God,
And a kind Providence,
Will enable me to confuse my tormentors
By her presence in a very few days.
It is only a question of time
Until she returns.

Emma Goldman
Stephanie Kuehnert

"If I can't dance,
I don't want to be a part of your revolution,"
Are words they like to print alongside my image.
I did not actually speak them,
But as an agitator who loved to dance,
Who believed that anarchy meant
Release and freedom of expression,
This misquotation does not trouble me.

Another error can be found on my headstone,
Where dates of both birth and death are listed wrong.
Though, again, what matters more,
Is my proximity to Albert, Lucy,
And the tribute to the Haymarket Martyrs,
Who had such a profound influence on me.
June 27, 1869 is my correct date of birth,
And Russia was the place my family called home.

My father believed that marriage
Was the proper path for Jewish girls,
Not education. But I would not let him stop me.
I studied the world around me,
Finding the Nihilists of particular interest.
Halfway through my sixteenth year,
I moved to New York and became a seamstress.

The events of Haymarket
Inspired my "spiritual birth and growth."
Along with meeting Alexander Berkman,
My friend, lover, and co-conspirator.
The ways we chose to support The Cause,
Especially our plot to assassinate anti-union industrialist,
Henry Clay Frick,
Were considered extreme,
Even by fellow anarchists.

But I found many different ways to fight,
For freedom and equality.
I took to the podium and the printing press,
My publication, *Mother Earth*,
Giving voice to free-thinkers around the world.
I agitated for contraception,
And stood against the draft.

Deported from the United States,
And disillusioned in Russia,
My life came to an end in Canada,
The year 1940, my age seventy.
Now, by the banks of the Des Plaines River,
Alongside so many other great activists,
My ghost dances with the revolutionaries
Who come to visit me.

William "Big Bill" Haywood
Amy Binns-Calvey

Only half of me is buried here,
Did you know that?
Other half's in Soviet Russia.
The evil scourge of capitalism,
Killed the dream of the Soviet Union.
But when I was still there
The dream of a worker's state,
Where all men and women are equal,
Was still alive.
Half of me's in the Kremlin wall,
And the other half here,
By the Haymarket martyrs.

Guess you want to know,
About my past and all that.
I was born in the Utah Territory.
I'm not a Mormon.
Though you couldn't swing a cat,
Without hittin' one when I was a kid.
Blinded my right eye when I was nine,
Whittlin' a slingshot.
Guess there's some sort of moral in there,
Limited perception.
Hate to think what would have happened,
If I had seen the whole amount of injustice in this world.

I was seventeen and working in a mine,
When the Haymarket massacre happened.
Innocent men hanged,
For trying to get justice for the worker.
I was twenty-five,
When the president of the United States,
Grover Cleveland,
Called in the army to end the Pullman strike.
Men and women who's wages were cut,
But rents in the company housing left the same,
Only trying to get what was fair,
Attacked by their country's army!

At twenty-seven, I heard a speech,
From the president of the Western Federation of Miners,
And I joined right up.
Didn't take me long to see,
That the world needed one big union for everyone,
Regardless of race, skill, industry.
In Chicago,
I helped form the Industrial Workers of the World.
I spoke at the first convention,
"The aims and objects of this organization,
Shall be to put the working-class
In possession of the economic power, the means of life,
In control of the machinery of production and distribution,
Without regard to capitalist masters."
You can see why I ruffled some feathers.

In 1907 I was falsely accused of murder,
Framed by Pinkerton detective James McParland.
Good old Clarence Darrow got me out of that one.
I got some fame,
Was even called the "Lincoln of Labor."
Yeah, I shot off my mouth and got into some trouble.

Sounded like I was calling
For the workers to confiscate property,
And union organizers got arrested.
Well, like I said, the capitalist has no heart.
But if you harpoon him in the pocketbook,
You'll draw blood.

Became a Socialist,
Involved in strikes.
They finally got me during WWI.
Convicted of espionage,
Encouraging desertion, and avoiding the draft.
While I was on bail,
I left the U.S. for Russia.
In Russia, I was pretty high up with the movement,
Until Stalin.
Married me a Russian gal,
Though we couldn't speak each other's language.
I wished I could have stayed in America.

I'm sure you think
You got it solved now,
Workers' rights.
You all are pretty comfortable,
But I'll bet, with even my one eye,
I could see things as they really are.
As long as money is calling the shots,
There won't be justice for the workers.
Sometimes I wonder which half of me is where.
Guess I got enough righteous anger for both halves.

Oscar Neebe
Frances McNamara

I don't belong here.
I was pardoned,
I don't deserve it.
I tried to tell them that.
I tried to tell them to hang me.

I told the judge.
"I think it is more honorable,
To die suddenly,
Than to be killed by inches.
I have a family and children.
They can go to the grave,
And kneel down by the side of it.
But they can't go to the penitentiary,
And see their father,
Who was convicted for a crime,
That he hasn't had anything to do with."

They gave me fifteen years anyways.
Altgeld gave me a pardon.
By then, I didn't have the heart for it.
I retreated behind a bar.
As saloonkeeper,
A least I could serve a man and his family,
Some ham and cheese, a schooner of beer.
In peace.
For that, I don't deserve to be here.

Louis Lingg
Frances McNamara

I said,
"I despise you,
Despise your order, your laws,
Your force propped authority.
Hang me for it."
But not really.

You think I'd let them hang me,
And have the last word?
Not on your life.
Spies stopped the presses.
He took back the posters calling workers to action,
Telling them to bring weapons.

Bah! I said.
"When you hang us, they will throw the bombs!"
But you're not hanging me.
You kept finding the bombs in my cell.
But you couldn't stop me in the end.
You couldn't hang me.

I got a blasting cap passed to me, hah!
Stuck it in the side of my mouth,
Lit it up,
And Kaboom!

Only half my face was blown away.
The next six hours were agony.
Somehow I can't rid myself of the nagging memory,
Even now.
But you didn't hang me!
Victory!

Albert Parsons
Frances McNamara

An eight-hour day,
That was all we wanted.
It was the demonstration, the week before,
That was important.

The Haymarket meeting was just to protest
The police attack on the other demonstration.
Spies stopped those crazy posters, calling for weapons.
It was supposed to be just more talk.
Speeches, like always.
Even the mayor got bored and drifted home.

That was when I gathered up Lucy and the kids.
We went to Zeph's Hall on Lake Street,
For cold ham, cheese, bread,
A dark ale with a taste rich as a summer night.
I can still smell it.

A flash, boom, screams, and gunshots.
Who did it? Hot heads like Lingg?
But he wasn't there.
A set up? Does it matter?
None of us minded
Giving a life for what we believe in.
But it does seem it ought to be
For something you actually did.

No matter.
I couldn't let the others hang without me.
You'd think they might have
Let me have my last words at least.
But they sprung the trapdoor
Before I could finish my line.

And it was done.
Passing a law for an eight-hour workday,
That's the only victory worth having.

Lucy Parsons
Mark Rogovin

Mine, the tiniest of gravestones,
Reads Lucy Parsons, 1859 to 1942.
I am sheltered by the most magnificent monument,
The Haymarket Martyrs.

My husband was Albert R. Parsons,
One of three martyrs hanged in 1887,
Just north of downtown Chicago.
All were buried at our cemetery,
With over 15,000 taking the train to Forest Park,
To see us on our way.

I am buried alongside anarchists and communists,
Socialists and unaffiliated progressives,
Auto workers, union organizers, and writers.
I am close to foe, and then friend, Emma Goldman,
And William Z. Foster,
And twenty-two-year-old Ellen Budow.
Some of Joe Hill's ashes were scattered nearby,
And more folks were buried one month ago.

When Albert was hanged
I raised the money for the monument
And toured the nation,
Continuing my mission to support unions
And to work for the poor.

Oh, by the way,
There are still many plots available.
If you want to be buried alongside the Martyrs,
Or have your ashes scattered,
Just stop in at the office and sign up.

When you come to visit me,
Bring a piece of paper and crayons,
And do a rubbing.
And, when you leave,
Lay down a red rose.

Merlin

Frances McNamara

How quaint.
The United Ancient Order of the Druids.
"St. Merlin" for their patron.
Has a nice ring to it, don't you think?
Of course, these days spells are cast in ones and zeros.
We fight vicious worms and bots and spiders,
From fortress buildings packed full
With floor upon floor of blinking servers.
The fight goes on, in silence.

It's good to know there are still those devoted
To the principles of justice, benevolence and friendship,
"The Seven Precepts of Merlin"
(Whatever those are).
Fight for right,
The strong defend the weak,
That's the ticket!

For us immortals
It's touching to have a memorial in stone like that.
I look a little weary, though,
And in need of a barber, don't you think?
Ah, well, it's back to the front lines for me.
But keep up the good work.
Keep up the fight!

Louis Borodkin
Arnie Bernstein

In Russia, the Cossacks ran wild,
Looking for Jews to kill on orders from the Tsar.
They tore through our village.
I hid my family on the roof of our small house
And held my three-year old daughter's mouth closed,
So the madmen below would not hear her frightened cries
And discover us up above.

We joined thousands upon thousands of Jewish refugees
From Russia and the countries of Eastern Europe,
Fleeing our despotic homelands for sanctuary in America.
We came through Ellis Island
With other men, women, and children.
Immigrants from Greece, Italy, Sicily, Spain, Germany…
Poked, prodded, and processed by officials.
My wife, Elizabeth, and our children headed west
And settled in Chicago in the immigrant ghettos.

Halsted Street overflowed with people like us,
Exiles from their homes but, now,
In a new village within Chicago,
In a new century.
We were no longer Russians.
We were *Americans!*
I found a job.
Like many of my *landsmen* I became a pants presser,
Humble but steady work.

We were safe and far away
From the Tsar's anti-Semitic pogroms.
Yet, even in America, people saw us as Jews first.
Outsiders,
Still facing unspoken and unwritten rules
About who we were and what we could do.
There were places, even in America, land of the free,
Where Jews were not welcome.

But, upstairs, in a room of a nearby movie theater
On Roosevelt Road—The Central Park,
A real palace, run by four Jewish brothers,
Two named Balaban and two named Katz—
There was a sanctuary of a back room,
Where hardworking men like me,
Pants pressers, cigar rollers, rag peddlers,
Janitors, butchers, tailors,
Americans now, could gather,
Free from the burdens of everyday life.
We played cards,
Smoked fat cigars,
Ate sandwiches piled high with corned beef,
And played cards.

In 1914 we joined our Jewish brethren across the country
In a fraternal organization—
"The Progressive Order of the West."
Our Order raised money for charities—
The Hebrew Immigrant Aid Society,
The Jewish National Fund,
And other Jewish causes.
Plus, there were personal benefits—
Disability to man or woman: $500,
Death benefits: $500,
$50 more for funeral expenses.

We joined with other Hebrew burial societies in Chicago
And founded one of the many Jewish cemeteries
That run, like a patchwork,
In Forest Park, near Waldheim Cemetery.
Together our graveyards became known as "Jewish Waldheim."
(Even in death we are different.)

My name is on a plaque on the cemetery entrance,
As a member of the board of directors.
In the center of the cemetery,
Just off the main road,
Is a stone with the name "Borodkin" carved on the face.
In front of it is the grave of my wife, Elizabeth,
Who preceded me in death on February 23, 1950.
I joined her on May 6, 1958.
Eventually our son Milton joined us,
Along with our daughter Regina,
And her husband, Samuel Bernstein,
Another immigrant from Russia.
We are Americans at peace,
Far from the terror of the country we fled.

"Maria" The Palm Reader

Tracy Reynolds Aleksy

They will come for me this time,
The Kalderash.
To picnic in my memory,
As I have done for my forefathers.
They will bring the roast pig,
And the wine, the violins, and the guitars,
The children and the elders.

They will sing to me,
Drink with me,
Pray for me.
I will watch them,
The young girls dancing,
The young men smoking,
My brothers holding their cigarettes gingerly,
As their bows fly to hide their grief.

My sisters,
Beating their breasts, weeping,
And again cursing the fever,
That took me and so many others.
I did not "see" it,
As I saw so much,
In the lives of those who came to me,
For a glimpse into their futures.

What I read for them,
Was not in their palms,
But in the their dress,
Their questions.
And, especially, in their eyes.
Some were hopeful,
Some were frightened,
Some were dreaming.
Others, a few,
Were evil and menacing.

But all who came to me
Were given answers to their questions,
Resolution to their mysteries.
The only answer to mine was death.
In the papers they call it "influenza,"
And feed the frenzy of fear,
In those yet untouched.

But the Family will care for them,
And for those left behind,
Until we all are joined together,
Under the grass and stones.
And the ones who picnic in this place,
Of peace and silence,
Are strangers.

Eddie Balchowsky
John Rice

I've been fighting fascism my whole life.
It began in my hometown, Frankfort, Illinois.
Our family ran the general store,
We were the only Jews surrounded by German farmers.
When kids called me kike,
My mother told me to turn the other cheek.
I never turned the other cheek.

When I heard fascists were fighting
To overthrow Spain's democracy,
I put my hometown and Hitler together.
I said to my friends, "Let's go."
The government said we couldn't.
To hell with that.
Let them try and stop us.

I joined the Abraham Lincoln Brigade in '36.
There were 2,800 Americans who felt like me,
And we joined 35,000 freedom fighters,
From fifty-two countries.
The State Department prohibited us
From traveling to Spain.
We landed in Lisbon,
And hiked over the Pyrenees,
To face Franco and his thugs.

I had discovered the piano when I was six.
I later became a concert pianist,
Taking great liberties with Chopin.

Whenever I could find a piano in Spain,
I was banging on it.
In '37, Paul Robeson came to our camp.
He needed an accompanist.
I jumped up and played my heart out.

Not long after, we were digging in on a hill.
We hit solid rock.
When the sun came up,
My commander told me to leave my rifle
And fetch a barrel of coffee
And a bag of bread from the food truck.
When I stood up, all hell broke loose.

I was the first man hit.
A machine gun bullet got my right arm.
Two stretcher-bearers tried to reach me.
One was hit. The other told me to go down the hill.
Bleeding and confused,
I turned around and ran toward the top.

I was drawing fire,
So one of the Lincoln's pushed me,
And I rolled down the hill.
I found an ambulance.
There were eighty-five men on that hill.
I understand that not very many got off.

Three months in the hospital.
Got my right arm amputated
And was sent home.
The fascists took Madrid in '39.
We lost 750 Americans trying to stop them.
But we premature anti-fascists woke up the world.

I left an arm in Spain,
And came home with something in its place,
A morphine habit.
Having a stump made it real convenient to shoot heroin.
I wasn't taking liberties with Chopin anymore.
I was playing along with him using one hand.

I was still good,
Played for Tom Waits, Stan Getz, and David Bromberg.
I'm sure you've heard of The Mamas and the Papas.
I'd play weddings, too.
I spent my days drinking at the Quiet Knight in Old Town.
That place had a juke box, Beatles to Fats Waller.

Otherwise, I was shooting up in the alley.
The cops wouldn't leave me and my friends alone.
When their lights caught me,
I'd stick my stump in my mouth,
And walk a straight line.
The cops would laugh so hard
They couldn't hear their radio.
They'd tell me to get the hell out of there.

I was a good pool player and painter.
I did Corky Siegel's album cover.
Studs Terkel was my friend and filmed me,
In "The Good Fight,
The Abraham Lincoln Brigade in the Spanish Civil War."
At the premier in '85,
I played the piano onstage at the Biograph Theater.
Then I watched myself on screen.
I had dark curly hair and wore a beret.
My dark eyes stared out from my beard and moustache.
I asked my younger self,
"Where are you now that I need you?"

I was also filmed by the Today Show.
Flew me to that hill in Spain where I got hit.
I sang the same songs as me and my comrades sang.
"There's a valley in Spain called Jarama."

I did a lot of bartending,
Had a lot of friends:
Mother Blue and Junkie Ray and George Badonsky.
I took off for California in the 80s,
But couldn't stay away from Chicago.

I don't want to talk about the old days anymore.
It's too painful to think about,
Especially because it makes me think about myself.
Besides, I'm too caught up with my problems to think about it.
I'm glad I fought in Spain,
But, from then on, I fought only myself.

Charles Burroughs
Mark Rogovin

I was born in Brooklyn, New York.
In 1928 my mother, Williana,
Took me and my brother to the Soviet Union.
She was a teacher in New York City,
And a member of the Communist Party.

It's a little known fact that African Americans,
Who had sympathies with the early Soviet Union,
Emigrated there to teach farming
And other occupations.
So I was schooled there,
And loved the language,
Poets and all.

I had a special love for the Russian poet Pushkin,
And spoke by memory his lines,
In my gravelly bass-baritone voice.

> *Good For the Poet Who...*

Good for the poet who applies,
His art in royal chambers' splendor,
Of tears and laughter crafty vendor,
Adding some truth to many lies,
He tickles the sated taste of lords
For more greatness and awards.

And decorates all their feasts,
Receiving clever praise as fees...
But, by the doors, so tall and stout,
On sides of stables and backyards,
The people, haunted by the guards,
Hark to this poet in a crowd.

In 1945, I was called by the draft
And came back to the United States.
I loved history and enrolled in Roosevelt University,
Studying American history,
And African-American history.

I married Margaret Goss
And, in 1961, we co-founded the DuSable Museum
Of African-American History.
We lived in a brownstone on Michigan Avenue,
And the living room and dining room
Became the first home of the museum.

In the basement we had workshops
For busloads of students.
I was the museum's first curator.
It was funny—
Margaret loved cats,
And they had the run of the displays.
In 1973 the museum moved to a large home
In Washington Park.

I could tell you about my published books,
Of poetry and more,
But it was the influence of the DuSable
That made life "worth it."

Please don't look hard for a gravestone.
Margaret scattered some of my ashes,
At the first home of the DuSable,
And the rest of my ashes,
In a ring around the Martyrs' monument...
And that is where my heroes are laid to rest.

Frank Lumpkin
Mark Rogovin

This is the story about me,
Frank Lumpkin.
I'm the son of Georgia cotton sharecroppers,
Who moved to the orange groves of Florida.
I became a professional boxer, construction worker,
Merchant seaman,
And last, a steelworker,
In Buffalo and Chicago.

I worked in Chicago's Wisconsin Steel for thirty years.
In 1980 thousands showed up for work,
And found the mill's entrances bolted shut!
No pay, no pensions!
I stepped forward,
And helped form the "Save Our Jobs Committee."
We picketed in downtown Chicago
And took a bus to lobby
In the halls of Congress.

"Re-Open Wisconsin Steel,"
"Justice for the Wisconsin Steelworkers,"
"Pay the Wisconsin Steelworkers,"
It was a question of fight in solidarity. Or die!
And after seventeen years of struggle—
We won!

Studs Terkel said of me,
"You are one of my heroes—
You give me, and millions of others, much hope.
You are a true progressive workingman,
In the best sense of the word…
And a leader. With admiration."

My gravestone is seventy feet south of the Haymarket Martyrs.
Below my name, birth, and death dates it concludes,
"Communist."

Joseph C. Corbin
John Rice

Call me Carpetbagger,
I'm sure many did.
I prefer a different title, Educator.
I'm Joseph Carter Corbin,
Professor J. C. Corbin to many.

I was born a free man of color,
In Chillicothe, Ohio.
It was 1833 and millions were still in slavery.
There were no schools for the Colored—
As we were called in polite circles,
In the so-called free state of Ohio—
So I was home-schooled.

At seventeen I enrolled at Ohio University.
I was the third African-American student
To walk the campus at Athens.
It took me a mere three years
To get my bachelor's degree in art.
I went back two more times, in 1856 and 1889,
To earn master's degrees.

Reconstruction came along,
And there were new opportunities
For people of color.
I moved my family to Little Rock, Arkansas,
Where I got a job as a newspaper reporter.

The Republicans were in power
And I made some good connections.
I was elected to state office—
Superintendent of Public Instruction.
Not bad for a carpet-bagging man of color.

I worked on legislation
To create a college for black students.
But, with the victory of the Democrats,
In the election of 1874,
Reconstruction came to an end,
And I got forced out as Superintendent.

I wanted black students to become educated,
Not just to train for industrial jobs,
Or to be domestics.
The people in power didn't.

But I never forgot my dream of starting a college
For Arkansas's black students.
I found an ally in Governor Garland,
Who encouraged me to open Branch Normal College.
I'm proud to say it's now called
The University of Arkansas at Pine Bluff.

In my day at Branch Normal,
Black students could take classes
And learn vocational skills.
We started with seven students…
By 1894 we had 241.
There was a two-story brick building with classrooms,
An assembly hall, an industrial department,
And a dormitory for girls.

I was highly educated myself,
And could speak and read eight languages,
Including Danish.
I taught Greek and Latin at Branch Normal,
Showed students how to play the piano, organ, and flute,
Started the first school band,
And directed the Normal School Choir.

After I retired, my wife and I moved
To Bronzeville, on the South Side of Chicago.
I passed away in Pine Bluff, Arkansas
On January 9, 1911.

They buried me here in the family plot at Forest Home,
Next to my wife and sons.
Call me carpetbagger if you want.
I've been called worse.

Smiley

Robert K. Elder

We all love the spotlight,
But it's only so big.
And it only lasts for so long.
Let me show you this,
With a story that is mostly true.

In the early morning of June 22, 1918,
A train engineer fell asleep.
He did not see the red light
Of the first signal,
Nor the second.
A frantic flagman was a blur.
So, at 3:56 a.m.,
Near Hammond, Indiana,
The engineer slammed into the sleeping cars
Of the Hagenbeck-Wallace Circus train.
The grinding roar
Sounded as if a million bricks
Were crashing into a tin roof.
Then, silence.

In thirty-five seconds,
Eighty-six people lost their lives.
The final count is uncertain,
Because some roustabouts we took on
In Michigan City
May not have made it onto the payroll.

A fire raged through the wreckage,
Taking with it those
Who were pinned under the debris.
Nearly one hundred thirty were injured.
Our strongman, Arthur Dierckx, died.
We lost Jennie Ward Todd of the famous Flying Wards,
A family trapeze act.
Many of the dead couldn't be named.

The crash was so catastrophic,
And the dead so burned beyond recognition,
That man could not be separated from beast.
Trainers, elephants, horses, workmen,
Clowns, aerialists, and midway stars
All died together.
So our remains were buried together,
In Showmen's Rest,
A section of Woodlawn Cemetery,
Purchased by the Showmen's League of America,
Under its first president, Buffalo Bill Cody.

It's a tragic story,
But one with a poetic end—
Man and animal buried together,
Bound in eternity,
In the brotherhood of the circus.

But I told you my story was mostly true.
And it's here,
On this final detail,
That the story crosses into legend.
It's a better story, but not true.
Yes, an estimated eighty-six of us died that day,

And most of us were buried at Showmen's Rest—
But not with circus animals.
The engine struck our sleeping cars,
Not the cages.
But I prefer the version I told you first.

This is true, however—
Many of us were buried without names.
Some among us only have headstones that read
"Unidentified Male" or "Unidentified Female."
Some kind soul was able to identify me
By my clown name, "Smiley."
A few other headstones read "Baldy,"
And "4 Horse Driver."
I've been asked to speak for us all,
To ask you not to forget us.

Across the street from our final resting place
Is a shopping mall—
Which, in many ways,
Has replaced the modern circus.
Each institution has freaks,
Nickel-grabbers, and carnival barkers,
All of them carried on a wave,
Of children screeching and laughing.

From here, just out of the spotlight,
We can almost hear them.
A few of them even visit us,
Attracted by the stone elephants that mark our graves.
This winter, a little boy walking
On the knobby, frozen ground above us
Said, "I think I can feel their bones!"
What imagination!
What flair for the fantastic!
He may grow up to be a ringmaster.

How we remember things matter,
Even if it's not all true—
Because there's still truth in it.
Even if it's a first name, like mine.
The show must go on—
Even if it's without us.

Billy Sunday
Michael Conklin

My grave draws only a few visitors,
Here in Forest Home Cemetery.
Perhaps they are curious,
Simply because a single word, "Sunday,"
Is etched in large letters at the top of the tombstone.

My detractors, and there were many,
Would find it amusing,
That I attract such a small crowd.
After all, millions came to hear me speak
At my revivals a hundred years ago—
About God, Jesus Christ, and temperance.

I was an old-fashioned preacher of old-time religion.
My message always was simple—
I believed the Bible is the word of God,
From cover to cover.
I was as comfortable on the kerosene trail,
In towns without electricity,
As I was in packed stadiums.

I dined in the White House with presidents,
Conferred with prominent businessmen,
Visited with Hollywood stars,
And donated thousands to charities.
I built a family compound in Indiana,
That became a national attraction for my message,
When I was not delivering it in our country's cities,
Great and small.

I was the sworn, eternal and uncompromising,
Enemy of the liquor traffic.
My favorite sermon was "Get on The Water Wagon."
Historians say I was the catalyst
For the Temperance movement
That ushered in Prohibition.

For that, I earned lifelong enemies.
To them, I offer this challenge—
Show me where the saloon has ever helped
Business, education, church, morals,
Or anything we hold dear.
In the beginning, I am sure crowds,
As small as they were,
Came to hear me because I was a novelty.
I was the Iowa farm boy raised in an orphanage,
Who gave up a major league baseball career,
And big money, to spread the Word.

I played eight seasons in the big leagues,
And five were right here in Chicago,
For our National League team.
We won championships.
My speed in the outfield
Was considered to be the best in baseball.
But I discovered the sport
Was only a triple in my life.

I really never touched home plate,
Until the off-day in 1887,
When I wandered into Chicago's Pacific Garden Mission.

It was there I first heard the Word of the Lord,
Became inspired to spread the Gospel,
Became an ordained Presbyterian preacher,
And, like any athlete,
Worked at my God-given calling.

By following Christ,
You may discover a gold mine of ability
That you never dreamed of possessing.
When conversion compels people
To forsake their previous calling,
I discovered God gives them a better job.

Without the benefit of TV, radio, and computers,
Over a hundred years ago,
I had less chance than anyone today,
To become a religious symbol in America.
Yet 3,500 persons attended my 1935 funeral,
In the Moody Church in Chicago.

I was buried here in Forest Park,
And, though not many people come
To see my eternal resting place,
This does not concern me, Billy Sunday.
If my story can inspire only one person
My message lives without me.
I can ask no more.
Or, as it says in the inscription
Farther down my tombstone:
I Have Fought a Good Fight,
I Have Finished My Course,
I Have Kept the Faith,
II Tim 4:7

Michael Todd
Robert K. Elder

When a friend complimented me
On "Around the World in 80 Days,"
Which was roaring its way through the box office
To win the Best Picture of 1956,
He said, "It's quite a movie, Mike."
As the film's producer, I told him,
"Bite your tongue when you call it a movie.
It's a '*show*.'"

You see, for a show
You need mystique, failure, redemption,
Passion, triumph, and drama.
That's a *show*.

Let's start with *mystique*.
And get a couple things out of the way:
I was Elizabeth Taylor's third husband,
And my name is not really Michael Todd.
It's Avron Hirsch Goldbogen.
My rabbi father knew me all too well.
Even when I was a child he would ask,
"What goes on behind those *gnaivishe eigen?*"
That was his way of saying "cunning eyes."
Maybe it's because I got kicked out of the sixth grade
For running a craps game.
But it probably started before that.

I knew that in a world of Christian names,
A more Americanized moniker like Mike Todd
Might serve me better,
As a producer of entertainment.

Failure. Yep, had my share.
And before Lizzie, I earned, and then lost,
A fortune in the construction business.
I founded a bricklayers' college that didn't stack up.
And later, when I started producing vaudeville,
And shows on Broadway,
I was the Boy Failure
Before I was the Boy Wonder.
Some dismissed me as a vulgar, cigar-biting carnival barker.
But Damon Runyon said I was
"The greatest natural gambler" he'd ever known.
You see, I knew the secret song of risk and reward.
Money is only important to people who haven't got it.
I was never poor, only broke.
Being poor is a state of mind.
Being broke is a temporary situation.
I was an artist—not a bookkeeper.

Redemption.
I struck gold with the "Moth and Flame" dance
At the Chicago's World Fair in 1933.
This risqué little number involved a dance
By a scantily clad young ballerina
Named Muriel Page.
During the finale
I'd burn off most of her costume,
With an artfully directed burst of gas.
A friend asked me,
"What girl wouldn't walk through fire for you, Mike?"

Passion.
Now we get back to Lizzie.
It was after I stormed Broadway,
And I was producing "Around the World in 80 Days,"
That I started courting her.
I was her third husband.
But, to be fair,
Lizzie was also my third wife.
For our engagement
I gave her a $100,000 diamond ring
And, for a wedding present,
I gave her two Chicago movie houses.
You can still see the facades today—
They're part of the Goodman Theater.

And *triumph.*
For "Around the World in 80 Days"
We shot in thirty-two foreign locations
And on one-hundred-forty sets.
We had Frank Sinatra, Marlene Dietrich,
Shirley MacLaine, and Noel Coward.
Lizzie was on my arm at the Academy Awards,
When "80 Days" beat out her film, "Giant,"
Then "The Ten Commandments" for Best Picture.
Can you imagine that?
Not only did we take down James Dean,
And my beautiful matinee-idol wife,
But I beat Moses.
Do you know how hard it is for a Jew to beat Moses?
In total, "Around the World in 80 Days"
Took home five Oscars.
Time magazine wrote that it was
"Brassy, extravagant, long-winded, and funny."
But they could have been talking about me.

There was *drama*, but the good kind.
A little while later, Lizzie and I had a baby girl together
And named her Elizabeth Frances.
We called her Liza.
I had the picture of the year,
The bride of the year,
And the baby of the year.
What more could a man want?

Lizzie and I loved one another deeply,
Though we were famous for passionate, public fights—
Long before anyone knew the name Richard Burton.
But ignore my posthumous jealously.
I will leave it at: I loved her.

And we did not have enough time together.
I died in a plane crash with my biographer, Art Cohn,
Aboard a twin-engine Lockheed Lodestar
That I christened *The Lucky Liz*.

In a year, Lizzie and I had a lifetime.
I was the only husband she did not divorce.
It was a good life, cut too short.
But, oh boy, it wasn't just a life—
It was a *show!*

Clara Peller
Amy Binns-Calvey

"Where's the what?"
That's what I said to them at first.
I can't hear so good,
And to be honest,
I didn't get it at first.
There was a piece of meat right there,
You could see it.
I wanted to say,
"There! There's the beef!"
I don't remember what the original line
Was supposed to be,
They kept trying to get me to say it.
I had emphysema
And couldn't say the whole line.
It sure wasn't as catchy as what I did say.
They had to poke me
When it was my time to say the line,
On account of I couldn't hear, like I said.
Some guy was scrunched down,
On the floor next to me,
Pulling on my dress.
But, oh honey,
Did I make money for those three words!

I don't know how the hell old I am!
Who cares!
New York Times says I was eighty-six when I died,
Other places say I was eighty-five. Big deal.

I was born in Russia.
Who kept records in 1902 in Russia?
I could've been born in 1900 for all I know,
At the turn of the century!
I don't know.
I told them at Social Security—
"I'll be whatever age gets me Social Security benefits."
I came over in 1905.
Do you think they cared if I was three of four or five?
I'm tiny, I probably looked like a toddler!

Oh, I don't know how much money I made.
Wendy's said half a million,
I don't think so.
It couldn't have been that much,
But who knows.
It's crazy, making all that money for a job
Where you're pampered and treated like a star.
Did you know they got free food all day long,
When you make a commercial?
They bring a chair over to you,
To sit on, in between takes.

You know, honey,
Before my big break,
I worked as a manicurist.
Now that's hard work,
That's the work they should pay you the big bucks for,
Holding women's hands,
Listening to their complaints—
"My daughter-in-law hates me…"
"He knows I hate roses…"
Ugh! I raised two kids on my own
During the Depression.

That's hard work,
That's what should have earned me the fame.
Dumb decision
To divorce at the beginning of a depression,
I can tell you.

No, I scrape and scrounge for years,
And, then, when I'm in my 80s,
I say three words and "bang!"
I'm rolling in the dough.
Wendy's fired me,
Because I made a Prego commercial.
How the hell can a spaghetti sauce threaten a burger joint?!
Ah, who cares.
I went on a lot of TV shows, coupla movies.
It was a blast.
And Wendy's lost a lot of money
After they stopped using my commercials,
So there!
I was glad to have some money to pass on to my grandkids,
Kids, especially my daughter.

Hey, would 'ya do me a favor?
Would you go check my headstone,
Make sure they didn't put "Where's the Beef!" on it.
I'm glad I said it, but, you know,
I did more than that.

Michael Caulfield
Michael A. Black

All I ever wanted to be was a cop.
As a kid, playing with my friends,
"What you wanna be when you grow up?"
Kids say lots of things…
A cowboy, an astronaut, a baseball player.
I already knew.
I wanted to wear the badge,
Drive a squad car, and help people in need.
It was my dream.
And some dreams do come true.
I finished high school,
Graduated from college,
And became a police officer
With the Forest Park Police Department.
I was twenty-two years old
And had my whole life ahead of me.
I was living my dream.

September 30, 1982.
Midnight shift on the police department.
Cool September night…
Mild fatigue. Up late.
The rest of the world is sleeping…
Thinking about getting off and going to sleep…
Thinking about what I'm going to do in the morning.
But it already *is* morning, isn't it?
It's after midnight,
The bewitching hour.

I'm with my training officer, James McNally.
We make what appears to be a routine warrant arrest—
Orin Dominguez, wanted by Chicago PD.
The initial arrest goes without incident,
But, as they said in the police academy,
Nothing is ever really "routine."

We unhandcuff Dominguez in the interrogation room.
His eyes flash,
As he sits back and rubs his wrists.
Been here before, man.
Twenty-six times before—
Burglary, narcotics, robbery.
Another officer, James Sebastian,
Brings a second prisoner into the room.
Dominguez mumbles something,
Getting to his feet.
One heartbeat.
"Sit down," McNally tells him.
Dominguez jumps forward,
Grabbing the pistol from Officer Sebastian's holster.
The first round, going off in a small enclosed room,
Is both startling and terrifying.
One bullet strikes Officer Sebastian in the foot.
The pistol roars again.
My world goes black as the bullet hits my head.

Another shot!
It hits McNally in the chest,
Striking his badge.
Miraculously, the bullet ricochets off his star,
And digs into McNally's arm.
He draws his weapon.
Dominguez continues to pull the trigger.
Another gun is on the floor!
My gun! He grabs it…one in each hand.

More shots.
The second prisoner,
Who's been brought in for a minor infraction,
Jumps toward Dominguez,
Who keeps pulling those triggers.
McNally aims his gun at Dominguez.
No easy shot.
Both my brother officers are bleeding.
I'm lying on the floor.
I can't move. Can't help.
God, please, don't let him miss.
McNally pulls the trigger.
I see the puff of smoke in slow motion,
As his bullet ends Dominguez's life.
Die, you son-of-a-bitch!

I'm watching all this from above now...
At my funeral I look down from heaven,
See two hundred police vehicles form a motorcade.
I wish I could tell them it's all right,
It wasn't their fault, this is a better place.
And I got to live my dream,
And know one thing for sure,
Michael Caulfield was a cop.

Paul and Barry Winder

Amy Binns-Calvey

Paul

I didn't want to go to that dumb show,
Mother made me.
She thought my brother Barry
Was too young to go on his own.
I told her,
"The theater is absolutely fireproof."
That's what it said in all the papers,
"Absolutely fireproof."

It was crowded with kids and mothers.
No place for someone about to be a man,
Like me.
We had tickets up top,
The cheap tickets,
No, the cheapest tickets.
Barry and me,
We tried to sneak down
To the more expensive seats.
Jerks put up a locked gate.
We had to go back to our crummy cheap seats.

I couldn't see a thing
Except an aerialist,
With a basket of flower petals
To drop on the kids,
Below in the audience.

Then there was a spark.
They all gasped,
The moms and little kids,
Like they thought
Something incredible was going to happen.

It didn't look right to me.
Pieces of scenery, burning, on fire,
Dropped to the stage.
I looked around,
Didn't see any exit signs.
They were turned off during the show
And curtains covered the doors.
There was panic.
I knew I had to keep my head.

Eddie Foy tried to calm the crowd.
He almost got hit with burning scenery.
I could tell he was scared
And he asked for the asbestos curtain
To come down.
Then the curtain got stuck,
And I made eye contact with the fairy,
Stuck above the crowd.
She dropped her basket of flowers
And the lights went out.

I grabbed Barry's hand.
Mother had told me not to lose Barry.
We fought to find a door out.
Some of the doors weren't doors,
They were windows painted
To look like doors.

We saw people by other doors,
But they couldn't figure out the locks.
The other doors opened in.
So many people were pushing to get out,
They jammed the doors.

They wouldn't back up.
I yelled,
"Back up so we can open the door."
But they couldn't hear.
It was so hot.
I found a fire escape,
But there were no stairs,
Just a platform.
We were one hundred feet above the ground,
With no goddamn stairs.

In the alley below,
There was a pile of people
Who had already jumped,
Or been pushed.
I told Barry not to look down.
The college students across the alley,
Built a bridge out of a ladder and planks.
That's the kind of college man I'd be,
If I could've.

Barry wouldn't budge,
He was scared.
I wouldn't leave Barry,
Mother would kill me.

♦

Barry

I couldn't wait to see Mr. Bluebeard.
There were over two hundred actors in the show,
And Eddie Foy,
And the theater was brand new,
And it was my Christmas present,
And Eddie Foy!
And the costumes and the sets,
Gosh a-mighty!

Don't tell Mother I said that.
She'd be mad,
Almost cursing, she'd say.
But gosh a-mighty, it was something.
Standing room only!
More than standing room,
People sitting on the floor, in the aisles.

Paul and me,
We tried to sneak down
To the more expensive seats.
We went down the stairway.
There was a big gate with a lock,
Had to go back to our original seats.

I could see okay.
I could see an actress,
Dressed like a fairy,
Waiting up in the air over the audience.
Then, there was this spark,
Up overhead.
Something incredible was going to happen.
Like a magic act,
Or a fire-breathing dragon.

People next to us
Started to leave.
But I wanted to see
What was going to happen next.
And then Eddie Foy came out!
But...he wasn't so funny...
He almost got hit with something on fire.
He told people to stay in their seats.
He said it would be okay,
They had a special fire curtain.

But the curtain got stuck,
And the lights went out.
I held Paul's hand,
Mother had told me to stay with Paul.
Everyone was climbing over chairs,
Screaming,
Some of those mothers were very strong,
And pushed really hard.
So many people were pushing to get out.

Behind us, a ball of fire
Whooshed through the theater.
Paul found us a door,
And he told me not to look down.
It was too scary,
I didn't like it.

Where am I now?
Do the doors to here open out?

Allen Holst
Kate Rufa

Who am I?
To you, probably no one.
A stranger, a number,
A sad statistic perhaps?
A grave no longer visited?
No. I am more…I was more.
I had feelings, hopes, and dreams. A story!

I am Allen Holst.
And while my story ended only thirteen years in,
It was mine. It was important.
I had parents who loved me.
I had a younger brother and two sisters—
My constant companions.

Everyone told me that my mother was beautiful.
I'm not sure I ever thought of her as beautiful,
But I remember her eyes were magic.
They could enchant you with their stare,
Or make you wither beneath a single icy glare.

My sisters looked very much like her.
But not their stares.
They never got to develop them.
They died with me, and I with her.

My father mourned for us,
In a small church in Forest Park.
Over a hundred years have passed,
And, yet, it still seems sad that he said goodbye,
Beneath cheerful Christmas decorations,
And a sign that boldly read,
"Peace on Earth, good will to men."
I don't think my father ever felt peace again.
I guess life's like that.

Oh, what I could have been?
I often dream about that…
If, indeed, ghosts may be said to dream.
What could I have been—
If the light at the Iroquois Theater never malfunctioned,
If I'd been able to make it to the fire escape
In a "fire-proof" building,
If the fire escape actually worked properly?
What would I have been,
If they had not borne my small and broken body,
Down the streets to my funeral?

Sadly, that part of my story was left unwritten.
Unfinished.
You see, I never had the chance to…
Watch an airplane fly,
Or know the gentle caresses of a girl,
Or even grow a beard.
Those things were stolen from me.
Would I have married, I wonder?
Grown handsome and strong?
Would I have gone to war or healed the sick?
That will never be known.

That's one thing we have in common, you and I.
No matter how many years may separate us,
We will always share this lack of knowledge,
My ending unwritten.
However, my time here is short,
Soon I must go.
Ghosts never linger very long.
But I was here,
And now you and I have been properly introduced,
Now you know who I am.
I am Allen Holst.
Remember me.
We are all here for such a short time.
When we part, our memory is all we leave behind.
So remember me,
Remember me, as I hope someone will remember you.

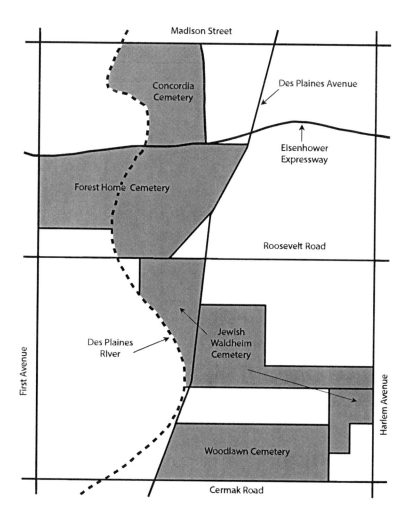

Madison Street

Concordia
Cemetery

Des Plaines Avenue

Eisenhower
Expressway

Forest Home Cemetery

Roosevelt Road

Des Plaines
River

Jewish
Waldheim
Cemetery

First Avenue

Harlem Avenue

Woodlawn Cemetery

Cermak Road

THE CEMETERIES OF FOREST PARK

A BRIEF HISTORY OF THE
CEMETERIES OF FOREST PARK

John Rice

Forest Park is home to five cemeteries, which include 680,000 graves. The town became a site for graveyards in part because of its geology. When the glacial "Lake Chicago" receded, a prehistoric sandbar formed. This elevated the land above the surrounding prairie, which later made it an attractive location for Native American settlement. In addition, the resulting soil was discovered to be ideal for digging graves.

The site where Forest Home Cemetery is now located was once a thriving village populated by members of the Potawatomi tribe. In the early 1830s these Native Americans were removed from their lands by the United States government. In 1839, President Van Buren gave a land grant of some of their former lands to a French-Indian fur trapper, Leon Bourassa.

In 1851, Ferdinand Haase, an immigrant from Prussia, purchased forty acres on the east side of the Des Plaines River from Bourassa. He constructed a home and began farming and grazing cattle. He also mined the property for gravel, which was carried away by a newly-constructed railroad spur. Haase opened a picnic ground called Haase's Park, capitalizing on the natural beauty of the parcel, and its easy accessibility by railroad and streetcar. A portion of the property was also used as a family burial plot. Haase's brother-in-law, Carl Zimmerman, passed away in 1854 and became the first non-Native American to be buried in what later became Forest Home Cemetery. Haase was prompted to open a cemetery after the city of Chicago closed the City Cemetery and placed a ban on future burial grounds within the city limits.

The first cemetery established in Forest Park was Jewish Waldheim Cemetery, which was founded in 1870 by an organization of synagogues. This sprawling cemetery is located south of Roosevelt Road and spans Des Plaines Avenue. It includes over 250 separate sections, representing individual congregations and other organizations.

Concordia Cemetery was established in 1872, when seven Lutheran churches from Chicago purchased land on the north side of what is now Forest Park. It is home to victims of the *Eastland* disaster, which is memorialized in an engraving of the ill-fated ship on the headstone of two of the victims. A small cemetery adjacent to Concordia is the final resting place of residents of the Altenheim–German Old People's Home.

In 1873, Haase sold a section of his property to an organization of German Masonic Lodges, who formed German Waldheim Cemetery. He then opened Forest Home Cemetery in 1876, on property adjacent to German Waldheim. He patterned it after Spring Grove Cemetery in Ohio, an example of a "rural cemetery," which featured large reflecting lakes and winding, tree-lined roads.

Waldheim and Forest Home welcomed all, regardless of their religious affiliation or ethnicity. This made the cemeteries very popular, not only with prominent local citizens, but also with immigrants and outcasts of all kinds. Among their many attractions are Roma graves located near the front entrance, the Haymarket Martyr's Monument and Radical Row, and the graves of several hundred Civil War veterans. Assorted labor organizations and fraternal organizations also have plots within the cemetery.

In the mid–1950s the construction zone for the Eisenhower Expressway cut through the south end of Concordia Cemetery and the north end of Forest Home Cemetery, prompting the removal of over 3,000 graves. All known descendants of the deceased had to be notified of the removals, and the resulting delay caused this section of the expressway to be the last completed.

In 1968, Forest Home and German Waldheim cemeteries merged, retaining the Forest Home name. Ferdinand Haase's New Orleans's style mansion was torn down, as was Forest Home's grand entrance, to be replaced by apartment buildings.

Forest Park's newest burial ground is Woodlawn Cemetery, established in 1912. It includes a section called Showmen's Rest, where fifty-six victims of a 1918 circus train wreck are interred in a mass grave. The Showmen's League of America, founded by Buffalo Bill Cody, had purchased the plot only a month before the horrific accident. It is marked by sculptures of elephants, their trunks lowered in mourning.

Many businesses developed around the village's cemeteries over the years, including taverns, restaurants, monument shops, and florists. Visitors flock to Forest Park's cemeteries to soak up their history, admire their monuments, and relax in their park-like settings.

CHARACTER BIOGRAPHIES

compiled by Jean Lotus

Eddie Balchowsky (1916–1989)
Soldier, artist, poet, pianist

Balchowsky grew up in Frankfort, Illinois as a member of the only Jewish family in town. During the Spanish Civil War he went to Spain to fight as a member of the Abraham Lincoln Brigade. In that conflict he lost an arm to machine gun fire. He was a concert level pianist who continued to perform with only one arm at Chicago clubs such as the Quiet Knight and Cross Currents. He was also a poet and painter whose paintings were exhibited at the Art Institute. He died after being struck by a Chicago subway train. [Forest Home Cemetery]

Philander Walker Barclay (1878–1940)
Photo-historian, bicycle repairman

Barclay moved to Oak Park, Illinois as a young teen. His father ran a drugstore in that town until 1902. With photography as his avocation, Barclay rode his bicycle through the region, obsessively photographing the homes, businesses, and people of Oak Park and River Forest. His collection of more than one thousand images is housed at the Historical Society of Oak Park and River Forest. [Forest Home Cemetery]

Louis Borodkin (1880–1958)
Founder of the Jewish Waldheim Cemeteries

Borodkin and his wife, Elizabeth, came to Chicago from Russia, fleeing the late nineteenth century pogroms. He helped run an immigrant-aid society, the Progressive Order of the West. He was also a director and founder of one of Forest Park's Jewish cemeteries, which later became the Jewish Waldheim Cemeteries. Borodkin was the great-grandfather and namesake of the author Arnie Bernstein. [Jewish Waldheim Cemetery]

Charles Burroughs (1919–1994)
Co-founder of the DuSable Museum of African–American History

Burroughs was born in Brooklyn, New York, but raised in the Soviet Union. He retained his U.S. citizenship and was drafted into the U.S. Army in 1943. After the war he came to Chicago, where he graduated from Roosevelt University. In 1961, he and his wife, Margaret Burroughs, co-founded the DuSable Museum. It was originally called the Ebony Museum of Negro History and Art, and was located in the Burroughs's living room in Chicago's Bronzeville neighborhood. The museum eventually moved to its current location in Hyde Park. Some of his ashes are scattered at the Haymarket Monument. [Forest Home Cemetery]

Michael Caulfield (1960–1982)
Forest Park police officer

Caulfield grew up in Oak Park, Illinois. After just a month on the job as a Forest Park police officer, Caulfield was shot and killed on September 30, 1982, when a prisoner in custody at the police department snatched his sidearm and opened fire.
[Mt. Carmel Cemetery, Hillside]

Joseph C. Corbin (1833–1911)
African-American newspaper editor, educator

Corbin was born in Chillicothe, Ohio, the eldest son of free black parents. He graduated from Ohio University, Athens, with a BA in 1853, and an MA in art, in 1856. In 1866, Corbin married his wife, Mary J. Ward, in Cincinnati. They then moved to Little Rock, Arkansas where Corbin began work as a newspaper reporter. During Reconstruction, Corbin served as Arkansas's Superintendent of Public Instruction and was president of the University of Arkansas board of trustees. In 1898, he formed the first association for black teachers in the state. He later opened Branch Normal College of the Arkansas Industrial University, which later became the University of Arkansas at Pine Bluff. He died in Pine Bluff, Arkansas. [Forest Home Cemetery]

Emma Goldman (1869–1940)
Anarchist, feminist pioneer, publisher

Goldman was a major figure in the history of American radicalism and activism. She was born in Kaunas, Lithuania and came to the U.S. as a young woman. She became attracted to the anarchist movement after the Haymarket affair of 1886. She and her lover, Alexander Berkman, plotted to assassinate industrialist Henry Clay Frick, but Frick survived their attempt. Goldman founded the anarchist magazine *Mother Earth* in 1906. She was imprisoned several times during her lifetime for inciting riots during her speeches, encouraging young men to resist conscription, and illegally distributing information about birth control. She was deported to Russia in 1917, but protested Soviet violence and repression, which she wrote about in her book, *My Disillusionment in Russia*. She later lived in England and France. She supported the anarchists during the Spanish Civil War in 1936. She died of a stroke in Toronto, Canada. [Forest Home Cemetery]

Belle Gunness (1859–?)
Serial killer

Born in Norway, Gunness came to the United States as a servant in 1891. During her career as a murderess, she is said to have killed between twenty and forty people, including her first two husbands, her own children, and a series of boarders on her farm in La Porte, Indiana. She was said to be motivated to kill by desire for her victims' insurance money, and the need to eliminate witnesses. She lured lonely bachelors and widowers to her farm with advertisements in the matrimonial columns of Midwestern newspapers. Thirty-four men, and their cash, disappeared soon after arriving on the farm, and human remains were later found buried in the hog pen. In 1908, a fire razed the Gunness farmhouse. A headless woman's body was found in the ruins, but neighbors insisted it could not be Belle, who was almost six feet tall and weighed around two hundred pounds. The body was buried beside her children's graves. [Forest Home Cemetery]

Caroline Hancock Hall (1843–1895)
Grandmother of Ernest Hemingway

Caroline was the daughter of Alexander Hancock, a British sea captain. Her mother died when she was a child. In 1853, her father sailed his three-masted barque, *Elizabeth of Bristol*, from England to Australia, and then to Panama, with his three children. The family eventually settled in Dyersville, Iowa, where Hancock became the postmaster. In 1865, Caroline married Ernest Hall and the two moved to Chicago to start a cutlery business. They raised their three children in Oak Park, Illinois. Caroline was an accomplished pianist and painter. [Forest Home Cemetery]

William "Big Bill" Haywood (1869–1928)
Co-founder of the International Workers of the World

Haywood was born in Salt Lake City, Utah. He worked as a miner in the West and became interested in the labor movement and socialism. In 1904 he was a co-founder of the International Workers of the World in Chicago. In 1905, former Idaho governor Frank Steunenberg was killed by a bomb at his home in Caldwell, Idaho. Haywood and two other radical colleagues were falsely accused of the crime and forcibly extradited to Idaho. Clarence Darrow successfully defended Haywood in the 1907 murder trial. Haywood soon gained a national reputation and Eugene V. Debs coined the name "The Lincoln of Labor" for him. He moved to Russia in 1917 to become an adviser to Lenin and died in a Moscow hospital in 1928. Half of his ashes are buried in the Kremlin wall, the other half were scattered at the Haymarket Monument. [Forest Home Cemetery]

Dr. Clarence Hemingway (1871–1928)
Physician, father of Ernest Hemingway

Hemingway was born in Oak Park, Illinois. A graduate of Oak Park and River Forest High School, he then attended Oberlin College and Rush Medical College. He married Grace Hall in 1896 and is said to have delivered the couple's first baby, Marcelline, with forceps, himself, after the doctor on call had a heart attack. Clarence enjoyed hunting, fishing, and the outdoors, passions he passed on to his son Ernest. Health problems caused by angina pectoris and diabetes probably contributed to his death at age fifty-seven from a self-inflicted gunshot wound. [Forest Home Cemetery]

Grace Hall Hemingway (1871–1951)
Mother of Ernest Hemingway

Grace Hall was raised in Oak Park, Illinois. She studied voice in New York City under Louisa Cappianni and gave a concert at Madison Square Garden. In 1896, after giving up a potential opera career, she married Clarence Hemingway in Oak Park. In addition to raising six children, she was an accomplished painter and composer. She died in Memphis, Tennessee. [Forest Home Cemetery]

Allen Holst (1890–1903)
Victim of the Iroquois Theater Fire

Allen attended the holiday performance of the Drury Lane musical *Bluebeard* with his mother Mary A. Holst and his sisters Gertrude, age ten, and Amy, age eight, at the Iroquois Theater on December 30, 1903. A fire in the theater killed 605 people, including many children. The Holst family was seated in the ill-fated second balcony, where they were trapped and unable to reach the fire escape. All four perished, survived by Allen's father and six-month-old brother. [Forest Home Cemetery]

James C. Justin, Jr. (1895–1915)
and E. Mary Manthey (1893–1915)
Sweethearts, drowned in the *Eastland* disaster

Justin and Manthey were an engaged couple, among the 844 passengers and crew who drowned in the *Eastland* disaster, on the morning of July 24, 1915. The *Eastland* was a steamship chartered to take 2,400 employees from the Western Electric plant in Cicero, Illinois to a company picnic in Michigan City, Indiana. While docked in the Chicago River, the ship listed suddenly and capsized in twenty feet of water. Many of the victims were local residents. Justin and Manthey are buried together under a tombstone reading "Sweethearts: Died on the Eastland." [Concordia Cemetery]

Joseph Kettlestrings (1808–1883) and
Betty Kettlestrings (1803–1885)
Pioneer settlers, founders of Oak Ridge (later Oak Park), Illinois

The Kettlestrings immigrated from England in 1833, passing through Baltimore and eventually settling in Chicago, population 350. They pushed further west and purchased 173 acres on a ridge of dry land, filled with oak trees. This was originally called Kettlestrings Grove and, later, Oak Ridge. They had eleven children, of whom six survived. It was said of the Kettlestrings, who were famous for their hospitality, that, "The kettle was always on and the (latch) string was always out." [Forest Home Cemetery]

Louis Lingg (1864–1887)
Haymarket martyr

Lingg was born in Mannheim, Germany, then moved to Chicago in 1885, where he joined the International Carpenters and Joiners Union. Although Lingg was not present at the Haymarket Square bombing in May 1886, police later reportedly found two spherical bombs and four pipe bombs in his apartment. He was arrested after a showdown with a revolver and imprisoned for the Haymarket conspiracy. Lingg committed suicide in his cell by detonating a blasting cap in his mouth the morning before he was scheduled to hang for the Haymarket events. He is buried in Radical Row. [Forest Home Cemetery]

Adolph Louis Luetgert (1845–1899)
Sausage manufacturer, convicted spouse-killer

Luetgert was born in Westphalia (now Germany), the son of a tanner. At about age twenty he immigrated to New York. He eventually settled in Chicago, where he became a successful butcher and meat producer, and was known in Chicago as the "Sausage King." In 1897 he was accused of murdering his second wife, Louisa (née Bicknese), and dissolving her body in lye in one of his sausage vats at the A.L. Luetgert Sausage and Packing Company. A hung jury ended Luetgert's first trial, but he was convicted of murder after a second trial in 1898. He died in prison a year later. [Forest Home Cemetery]

Frank Lumpkin (1916–2010)
Chicago steel worker, labor activist

Lumpkin worked as a steel mill worker, first in Buffalo, New York, and then at the International Harvester plant on Chicago's southeast side for thirty years. When the plant closed suddenly in 1980, locking out hundreds of union steelworkers, Lumpkin, then sixty-four, led the Save Our Jobs Committee to fight for back pay and benefits lost to employees. After years of lawsuits, International Harvester workers got a settlement of $15 million. Twice, Lumpkin ran unsuccessfully for the state legislature, as an independent. He is buried near the Haymarket Monument. [Forest Home Cemetery]

"Maria" The Palm Reader
Fictional representative of Gypsies buried in Forest Home

Maria represents the Kalderash subgroup of the Romani ethnic group (commonly known as Gypsies). For many decades, Forest Home Cemetery, with its "everyone welcome" philosophy, was the only permitted final resting place of many Illinois Romani. The Romani people observe many unique and ancient customs relating to death and burial. Their gravesites are often visited, and decorated, by loved ones—who leave offerings of cups of coffee, bottles of alcohol, and coins. In 1986, Steve Evans, Chicago's "King of the Gypsies," and patriarch of a Midwestern Romani clan, was buried in Forest Home Cemetery.

Merlin

The United Ancient Order of the Druids, a fraternal organization, began in London in 1781. The first United States lodge was established in New York City in 1839. The tradesmen's society met to spread "truth, justice, and righteousness" through the *Seven Precepts of Merlin.* They also managed a burial fund, and a widows' and orphans' protection society for members. The group had 17,000 members in 1896, and 35,000 by 1923, but began to fizzle out in the 1930s and was defunct by the 1970s. The druid statue sits atop an octagonal pedestal, with gravesites of members of the order buried in a circle around the monument. [Forest Home Cemetery]

Oscar Neebe (1850–1916)
Haymarket anarchist

Neebe was an anarchist and a defendant in the Haymarket bombing trial in 1887. He was not present at Haymarket Square the day of the riots, but was arrested and tried for conspiracy because of his anarchist views. He was sentenced to fifteen years in prison. He was pardoned in 1893, along with the other Haymarket defendants, by Illinois governor John Peter Altgeld. Neebe is buried in Radical Row. [Forest Home Cemetery]

Lucy Parsons (1859–1942) and
Albert Parsons (1848–1886)
Anarchist activists, publishers, Haymarket martyr

Born in Texas, Albert Parsons fought for the Confederacy as a teenager. He later became a Republican and an activist for the rights of former slaves. Parsons married Lucy Gonzalez (whose birth date is listed as 1859 on her headstone, but is usually listed as 1853) in 1871, and the two came to Chicago the following year. Albert became a reporter for the *Chicago Times*, but was fired after giving a speech during the Great Railroad Strike of 1877. A champion of the cause of the eight-hour workday, Parsons launched an anarchist newspaper, *The Alarm*, in 1877. On May 1, 1886, Parsons, with his wife and two children, led 80,000 people down Michigan Avenue, during the world's first May Day parade, in support of the eight-hour day. The night of May 6, after speeches in Haymarket Square, someone threw a bomb into the crowd, and seven persons were killed. Parsons was arrested two months later in Wisconsin and charged with spreading radical ideas. He was hanged as a co-conspirator in the Haymarket affair with three other anarchists. Lucy carried on the Parsons legacy, speaking around the country, and helped form the International Workers of the World (IWW) in 1905. She died in a house fire in Chicago. Albert is buried in the Haymarket Memorial Monument and Lucy is buried nearby. [Forest Home Cemetery]

Clara Peller (1902–1987)
Television advertising star

Peller spent thirty-five years as a manicurist at a local Chicago beauty salon to support her two children. At age eighty she began a new career as a comic actor in television commercials, becoming the spokesman for the Wendy's "Where's the Beef" advertising campaign in 1984. Sales jumped at Wendy's and an executive exclaimed of the campaign, "With Clara we accomplished as much in five weeks as we did in fourteen and half years." She allegedly earned $500,000 with her famous tagline. [Jewish Waldheim Cemetery]

Potawatomi tribe

The Potawatomi tribe and their ancestors lived in what is now Forest Park and environs for many generations. They buried their dead along the east bank of the Des Plaines River, in the area that became Forest Home Cemetery. Des Plaines Avenue is known to have been an Indian trail. The Native Americans were removed from the area by the United States government in the early 1830s and forced to move west. President Martin Van Buren presented a land grant in 1839 to French-Indian trader Leon Bourassa, who had married a Potawatomi woman. According to legend she stayed behind to tend the graves of her ancestors. A stone monument marks the ancient grave mounds. [Forest Home Cemetery]

Smiley (?–1918)
Circus performer, Hagenbeck-Wallace Circus train wreck

Smiley was one of eighty-six circus performers and roustabouts who died on June 22, 1918 in the wreck of the Hagenbeck-Wallace Circus train, near Ivanhoe, Indiana. On the way to Hammond, the train made an emergency stop at four o'clock in the morning to cool down overheated machinery. Red lights were turned on to warn approaching trains, but the engineer of an empty oncoming troop train had fallen asleep. His train hit the circus train at full speed, the collision destroying three cars full of sleeping circus people. Others were trapped in the wreckage when a fire broke out. Approximately sixty train crash victims, many known only by nicknames, were buried in the 750-plot section known as Showman's Rest. [Woodlawn Cemetery]

Billy Sunday (1862–1935)
Baseball player, Christian evangelist

Sunday was a major league baseball player, signing with the Chicago White Stockings in 1883. After being injured he became the team's business manager. He experienced an instant conversion to evangelical Christianity in 1887 after hearing a Chicago street preacher from Pacific Gardens Mission. With the help of his wife, Nell, Sunday created an organization that, between 1907 and 1935, swept through the United States, preaching salvation in common sense words to more than one million people. [Forest Home Cemetery]

Michael Todd (1909–1958)
Theater and film producer, third husband of Elizabeth Taylor

Todd was born Avrom Hirsch Goldbogen, son of a Minneapolis rabbi. He made and lost his first fortune in a million-dollar Chicago construction business that went bust in 1930. He then moved to Hollywood, where he became a contractor at Hollywood studios. He was attracted to New York after producing the *Flame Dancer*, a risqué attraction at the 1933 Century of Progress. He eventually ended up on Broadway. Success there led him to Hollywood and a career as a film producer. In 1956 he won an Academy Award for Best Picture for his film *Around the World in 80 Days*. He married Elizabeth Taylor (her third of seven husbands, and the only one she didn't divorce) in 1954. He died when his private plane, a twin-engine Lockheed Lodestar, *Lucky Liz*, crashed in Grants, New Mexico. [Jewish Waldheim Cemetery]

Abraham Van Schoick (1836–1928)
Civil War veteran, Chicago streetcar driver

Van Schoick was born in Narrowsburg, New York, one of two sons of Dr. William Van Schoick. When the sons were conscripted into the Union Army, their father joined the unit as a physician and surgeon. After the war Abraham moved to Chicago, where he married his wife, Jennie, and became a streetcar operator. He moved to Forest Park when he retired and his family bible was given to the Forest Park Historical Society. [Forest Home Cemetery]

Paul (1886–1903) and Barry (1891–1903) Winder
Victims of the Iroquois Theater Fire

Brothers Paul and Barry Winder attended the holiday performance of the Drury Lane musical *Bluebeard* at the Iroquois Theater on December 30, 1903. A fire in the theater killed 605 people, including many children. The boys were seated in the ill-fated second balcony, where they were trapped and unable to reach the fire escape. Their bodies were identified by their father. [Forest Home Cemetery]

AUTHOR BIOGRAPHIES

Tracy Reynolds Aleksy, a health professional for over forty years, has flirted with prose and poetry writing even longer. When not in the grip of a fascinating mystery, she has been known to share the gift of reading with others through literacy tutoring. She lives with her well-known, award-winning bookseller spouse in Oak Park, Illinois.

Kathryn Atwood is the author of *Women Heroes of World War II* (2011) and editor of *Code Name Pauline: Memoirs of a World War II Special Agent* (2013), both of which were published by Chicago Review Press. She has been presenting her "History Singers" programs—a combination of musical performance and lecture regarding the history of American pop and folk song—with her husband, John, since 2003. *The Song of the Potawatomi* is part of their program titled "Chicago History in Song."

Donald Perrot is a member and elder of the Prairie Band Potawatomi Nation. He is a heritage fluent speaker of the Potawatomi language, one of only ten still alive. He has published numerous manuals on the language, and is a frequent guest teacher and lecturer.

Arnie Bernstein is the author of three books on Chicago history. His 2009 work *Bath Massacre: America's First School Bombing* (University of Michigan Press) was honored as a Notable Book of the Year by the State Library of Michigan. His most recent book is *Swastika Nation: Fritz Kuhn and the Rise and Fall of the German-American Bund* (St. Martin, 2013). He is a member of the

Society of Midland Authors, the Chicago Writers Association, the Authors Guild, and PEN. A native Chicagoan and lifelong White Sox fan, Arnie also teaches composition at Triton College and Morton College.

Amy Binns-Calvey is a co-author/original cast member of the long-running *Flanagan's Wake* and founding member of The Noble Fool Theater Company. She has directed *Flanagan's Wake* in many markets including off-Broadway, Boston, Cleveland, Buffalo, Philadelphia, and Muskogee, Oklahoma. Her directing credits include *The Spew, Outbursts, Mikado: Version 2.005, Open Call,* and the world premiere of *Ma Murphy's Chowder House.* Amy is also a co-author of the Christmas send-up *Roasting Chestnuts.* Her play, *The Naked Show,* has had several readings in Chicago and her newest work, *I Didn't Know George Gershwin Could Play the Piano,* recently had a reading in Oak Park, Illinois. Amy is a member of the Dramatists Guild of America and a Network Playwright with Chicago Dramatists.

Michael A. Black is the author of nineteen books and over one hundred short stories and articles. He has a BA in English from Northern Illinois University and an MFA in Fiction Writing from Columbia College Chicago. He was a decorated police officer in the south suburbs of Chicago for over thirty years and was awarded the Cook County Medal of Merit for his police service before his retirement in 2011. He has written two Chicago-based series, one featuring Ron Shade, a kickboxing private eye, and the other police procedurals featuring Frank Leal and Olivia Hart. His most current books are *Sleeping Dragons,* in Don Pendleton's The Executioner series (Gold Eagle, 2013), and *Pope's Last Case and Other Stories* (Dark Oak Mysteries, 2013).

Jay Bonansinga, a *New York Times* bestselling author (*The Walking Dead, Frozen, Shattered*), is also a busy screenwriter whose film work has been honored at numerous festivals, including the Queens International, Houston, Iowa City, and Chicago International

Film Festivals. He has been called "one of the most imaginative writers of thrillers" by the *Chicago Tribune* and is published in nine different languages. Jay's 2004 non-fiction debut, *The Sinking of the Eastland* (Citadel, 2004), won the Certificate of Merit from the Illinois State Historical Society and was made into a musical by the Tony award winning Lookingglass Theater Company. His feature film debut, *Stash* (based on a Cemetery Dance short), premiered in fifty million households in 2009 on On-Demand.

Michael Conklin is a DePaul University faculty member, after spending thirty-five years at the *Chicago Tribune* as a staff writer and daily columnist. Mike has an MA in Chicago Studies from Loyola University and teaches occasional courses on local history. In addition to the *Tribune*, his featured work has also appeared in numerous publications including the *New York Times*, *History Magazine*, and *The Encyclopedia of Chicago*. He lives on Chicago's North Shore and in Scottsdale, Arizona.

Robert K. Elder is an author, editor-in-chief of *Sun-Times Media Local*, and founder of Odd Hours Media. Studs Terkel called him "a journalist in the noblest tradition" in his introduction to Elder's book, *Last Words of the Executed* (University of Chicago Press, 2010). His work has appeared in the *New York Times*, *Chicago Tribune*, Salon.com, and many other outlets. Elder's sixth book is *The Best Film You've Never Seen* (Chicago Review Press, 2013). He lives with his wife and twins in Oak Park, Illinois.

Carol Hauswald is a Renaissance woman, who writes, edits, researches, and performs. As Lynn Homewood she creates magical mystery and young adult fiction. As Carol Hauswald, she's an Illinois-licensed, and gifted certified, educator and a former Illinois State *Those Who Excel* finalist, who conducts staff development workshops, such as "How to Add More Laugh to Your Life." As Mrs. Canople, she teaches kids of all ages how to improv their self-esteem through comedy classes, one laugh at a time. Ms. Hauswald has Masters and Certificate of Advanced

Study degrees from National Louis University.

Kenneth J. Knack was born and raised in Forest Park. Along with spending countless hours exploring the local cemeteries, he authored a history of Forest Park for the Arcadia *Images of America* series. He has served as a Forest Park auxiliary police officer for the past sixteen years, as well as Vice President for the Historical Society of Forest Park since 2011. He is currently completing his second Arcadia book, *Elmwood Park*, to coincide with that village's 2014 centennial. He lives in Elmwood Park, Illinois with his wife Diane.

Stephanie Kuehnert is the author of two young adult novels, *Ballads of Suburbia* (MTV Books, 2009), and *I Wanna Be Your Joey Ramone* (MTV Books, 2008). She has an MFA from Columbia College Chicago. She also writes for *Rookie* magazine and, before leaving Forest Park in 2013, was a columnist for the *Forest Park Review*. She currently lives in Seattle, Washington, but Forest Park will always be her hometown.

Richard Lindberg is a historian and award-winning author of sixteen published books of non-fiction dealing with aspects of Chicago history, true crime in the Windy City, sports, and ethnicity. A past president of the Society of Midland Authors, his most recent books include *Whiskey Breakfast: My Swedish Family, My American Life* (University of Minnesota Press, 2011) and *Heartland Serial Killers: Belle Gunness, Johann Hoch and Murder for Profit in Gaslight Era Chicago* (Northern Illinois University Press, 2011).

Robert Loerzel has been a professional journalist in the Chicago area for twenty-five years, winning more than thirty awards for his work. He has written for publications including *Chicago* magazine, the *Chicago Reader*, and Pioneer Press, reported on the air for Chicago Public Radio, and photographed concerts for *Rolling Stone* magazine and other media outlets. In 2003, the University of Illinois Press published his book *Alchemy of Bones: Chicago's Luetgert Murder Case of 1897*. He has been avidly working on another book ever since. He has served as the president of the Society of Midland Authors. He lives in Chicago's Uptown neighborhood.

Frances McNamara grew up in Boston, where her father served as Police Commissioner for ten years. She has degrees from Mount Holyoke and Simmons Colleges, and is a librarian at the University of Chicago. She is the author of the Emily Cabot mystery series (published by Allium Press) which is set in 1890s Chicago: *Death at the Fair, Death at Hull House, Death at Pullman, Death at Woods Hole,* and the forthcoming *Death at Chinatown.*

D. M. Pirrone is the *nom de plume* of Diane Piron-Gelman, a native of Chicago. She spent eighteen years in Chicago's professional non-Equity theatre scene, then switched careers to fiction writing, editing, and audiobook narration. Her debut mystery novel, *No Less In Blood* (Five Star), appeared in 2011. Ms. Piron-Gelman is a longtime member of Mystery Writers of America and Sisters in Crime. She lives on Chicago's Northwest Side with her husband and two sons.

John Rice is a private detective who has been writing newspaper articles and columns for twenty-five years. He also teaches English composition at St. Augustine College and the Paris Business College. He is a member of the Historical Society of Forest Park and conducts historic tours of Forest Home Cemetery. He lives in Forest Park, where he and his wife Diane raised four children.

Mark Rogovin studied at the Rhode Island School of Design and worked in Mexico with the last of the great muralists, David Alfaro Siqueiros. He received an MFA from the Art Institute of Chicago. In 1981 he co-founded the Peace Museum. He co-authored the book, *Mural Manual,* and three other documents. For the last decade his main focus has been "Radical Row" in Forest Home cemetery. He is the author of *The Day Will Come: Honoring Our Working Class Heroes, Stories of the Haymarket Martyrs and the Dedicated Men and Women Buried Alongside the Monument*

(Illinois Labor History Society, 2011). Rogovin lives with his wife Michelle in Forest Park.

Kate Rufa broke into publishing with the essay "A Sherlockian Scandal in Philosophy," which appeared in *Sherlock Holmes and Philosophy* (Open Court, 2011). She graduated Summa Cum Laude from Saint Xavier University in 2009 with a BA in Philosophy. She is currently working on several other writing projects. When not writing, Kate enjoys teaching women's self-defense classes and spending time with her husband and children.

Sheila Reynolds Trainor is a native Chicagoan. She is the middle triplet in a family of twelve children. She had an interest in writing from an early age, and took writing classes all through school and beyond. As a college professor, she published many non-fiction articles related to her field of education. She has turned her interest back to creative writing, with a particular interest in writing books and poetry for children, drawn from experiences with them as teacher, social worker, and counselor during a thirty-five year career.

Emily Clark Victorson is the owner/publisher of Allium Press of Chicago, which is based in Forest Park, where she has lived for over twenty years. She has degrees from Oberlin College and the University of Michigan and, prior to starting the press, worked as a librarian, historian, and book designer. She has published numerous articles and essays on aspects of Chicago's history in publications such as *Chicago History*, and *The Encyclopedia of Chicago*. Allium Press was founded in 2009 as a small, independent press and publishes literary fiction, historical fiction, mysteries, thrillers, and young adult fiction, all with a Chicago connection.

CPSIA information can be obtained
at www.ICGtesting.com
Printed in the USA
FFOW05n1935111013
2043FF